Behavior Matters

Behavior Matters

And a Long Term Approach
to Investing and Life

Jason Sherr

Copyright © 2012 by Jason Sherr.

Library of Congress Control Number: 2012901488
ISBN: Hardcover 978-1-4691-5761-0
      Softcover 978-1-4691-5760-3
      Ebook   978-1-4691-5762-7

All rights reserved. No part of this book may be reproduced or transmitted in any form or by any means, electronic or mechanical, including photocopying, recording, or by any information storage and retrieval system, without permission in writing from the copyright owner.

Any people depicted in stock imagery provided by Thinkstock are models, and such images are being used for illustrative purposes only.
Certain stock imagery © Thinkstock.

Print information available on the last page.

Rev. date: 01/26/2016

To order additional copies of this book, contact:
Xlibris
1-888-795-4274
www.Xlibris.com
Orders@Xlibris.com

Introduction

Why write a book on your approach to investing and planning? After more than 20 years since I began in the financial services industry, I thought it would be helpful to current and prospective clients to lay out my philosophy. I also think it would be helpful to have a quick reference guide to the items I feel are most important.

I am hopeful that this book will be a good educational resource for you. The book is structured as a series of articles and will be updated over time as I continue to learn more.

Contents

About Jason 1

Philosophy 7

Goals-Based Planning 13

Diversification Explained 17

I Talked to My Clients about… 25

I Talked to My Clients Part 2… 31

More examples of what I do for Clients 37

I Believe… 43

About Jason

About Jason

I was born and raised in a suburb of San Diego, California called El Cajon. My parents still live in the house we moved into when I was 5 years old. I had a good childhood, no major issues.

For the most part, my childhood revolved around baseball. I still love the game today and I coached 14 seasons at Corona Del Mar High in Newport Beach. I was the head JV coach for most of those seasons (1997-2010).

As is the case with most passions, I typically did something baseball related about every day. On the weekends, I spent even more time hitting, catching, throwing, running and everything else. I love the history of the game, the smell of the field, the feeling of catching a hard groundball. All of it. I also like the fact that baseball is one of the only team sports that is not a back and forth game like football or basketball. It is a bit different. Timed by outs, not a clock. The defense has the ball.

My parents were very supportive of me growing up. They really allowed me to become the person I am today. While they offered guidance, I never felt like they pushed me in any one direction. They never said you have to go to college, it was just understood. I was an excellent student and attended the University of California- Berkeley (UC Berkeley or CAL) where I graduated in 1992.

My sister is 10 years younger than I am so we had more of a "parent/child" relationship for a long time. We have good rapport and I am very proud of her. She now lives in the New York City area after graduating from the University of California- Santa Barbara.

I attended Kindergarten at Ballantine Elementary and then we moved. I went to Narranca Elementary for the first grade thru the 5th grade. I then started the Magnate program in 6th grade at Fuerte Elementary.

I moved to junior high at Emerald for 7th and 8th grade then went to Valhalla High for just my freshman year. I attended El Capitan High in Lakeside, CA from the 10th to 12th grade. Primarily this was a baseball related decision. Then, as I mentioned, I moved onto UC Berkeley (CAL) and graduated with a Bachelor's degree in Architecture.

As it relates to my career, school is not where you learn to be a good financial advisor to your clients. You learn a lot more being in the field. I am glad I approached things the way I did. I think college gave me a more well-rounded view on how to think which, at the end of the day, is the most important thing about getting a university education- learning how to think.

After graduating from CAL, I moved back to San Diego. I started working for an advisor who ran his own one man shop, worked for an advisor at Dean Witter "cold calling", and worked in a Wells Fargo Bank branch. I wanted to see the three primary areas to enter the business. Quickly, I realized that a larger firm made sense because of the additional support. Within a one man shop, if you did not know the answer to a client's question then you were a bit stuck. With the larger firm, there was always someone to ask.

My wife and I started dating after I returned to San Diego. We had initially met while we were both going to CAL but did not see each other then. Ironically, we both ended up working in the same Wells Fargo branch in San Diego. I am very fortunate to have a very supportive and loving family. Our daughter is the light of our life. I'm very proud to have both of them.

At the time I began in the early '90s, firms were not doing a lot of hiring so I decided to work for the Kaplan Educational Center. To those who are unfamiliar, Kaplan is the largest test prep company in the world. They are owned by the Washington Post. I started in the San Diego office as an enrollment rep and eventually became the San Diego center manager. I then become the manager for San Diego and Orange County. After that promotion, we moved up to Orange County. I then became manager of the western regional enrollment center out of Westwood. We handled enrollments for most of the west coast.

I commuted from Newport Beach to Westwood for about 6 months, which was brutal. I then realized after being with the Kaplan Educational Center for a few years that I really wanted to get back to being a financial advisor. Firms were hiring again in the mid 90's and so I started with Dean Witter and went through their training program. I was officially on my own as an advisor in December 1996.

I then made the move to Smith Barney in October 1997 and I was with Smith Barney for 13 years. Smith Barney was a great firm. I left Morgan Stanley Smith Barney in Sept 2010 to go to Wells Fargo Advisors.

Philosophy

Philosophy

In my over 20 years of being involved in the financial services industry, I have learned a lot and still plan on learning more. One of the most important things I have learned is that it is very critical to focus on only the things one can control. There are a lot of variables out there that certainly affect us but we can do very little about.

When it comes to investing, you can really only control four primary things:

1. How your assets are allocated
2. How you are diversified
3. How you behave- the most important point in my opinion
4. How much you are contributing/saving

You can control those areas 100% of the time. All of us, however, have the tendency to spend time worrying about the other set of criteria for which we have no control. Things on this list might include:

1. The economy
2. The market
3. Politics

Anyone who gives a market or economic outlook, is merely offering a guess. It does not matter how many charts they have or how fancy of a Power Point presentation they have, it is still a guess. No one truly knows what the market or the economy is going to do. But everyone has an opinion.

I think John Kenneth Galbraith (economist and author) said it best, "The function of economic forecasting is to make astrology look respectable."

To me, the most important piece of the puzzle is behavior. Most people have poor investment behavior. The tendency is to want to "buy" after something has done well and "sell" after it has done poorly. In reality, it is certainly better to "buy" when something is down and "sell" when it is higher. Easier said than done, I know.

Sometimes I liken investor behavior to someone who goes to a large department store during their sale, and says that they will come back after the sale is over to pay full price. No one would do that but that is, effectively, what most people do when it comes to investing.

Each year, there is a group within the industry called Dalbar that creates statistical analysis on investor behavior. They do a 20 year look back on the "average" US stock based mutual fund. We can all identify with the "average" fund. They then compare that return with shareholder return. Simply put, what is the actual return investors are getting based on their behavior? Consistently, the shareholders underperform their own investments by a significant margin. The "Buy High, Sell Low" syndrome.

Why do they underperform? Because, they buy after the fund does well and then sell after it does poorly.

Goals-Based Planning

Goals-Based Planning

The most important thing to realize about planning and strategy is that you have to consider a lot of different things such as social security, Medicare and all the cash flows. You then need to put all of those things together in a comprehensive plan. It is also crucial to understand that you should be mainly concerned with your "direction". Are you headed on the right path?

Goals-based planning is a better way to view your goals and objectives relative to your portfolio. There are a few issues within Investment Planning that need to be addressed.

Historically, the financial services industry has done a poor job of answering the client question, "How am I doing?" The typical response was that relative to some index, here is how you are doing. Of course, that index has nothing to do with your actual goals and objectives.

A goals-based planner measures your progress to your actual goals in regards to retirement, education, travel or any other goals that are meaningful to you. Customized planning has merit because it is tracking your progress towards the things that matter to you the most. Some specific examples might be $100,000 in net retirement income, education for your children, purchase of a vacation home, etc.

The second issue within planning is that it is done at a point in time. You write a big comprehensive plan and strategy. It is good for that moment and then six months later, you have to redo the entire plan. Many plans are past their "expiration" date. Having a plan that dynamically updates on a daily basis is more helpful and flexible. In effect, you are always able to have a sense of where you are relative to the goals you have set forth.

The last major issue within planning has to do with return assumptions. When I started in the business in the early 90's, advisors would still assume that you earned a static return each year say 8%. As we all know getting 8% per year and averaging 8% per year can be two very different things. Percentages can be misleading.

For example, if you start with $50,000 and are up 100% then you now have $100,000. Then if you are down 50% you are back to $50,000. However, your "average" return would be 25% (up 100%, down 50% averages to 25% per year in that two year period).

Goals- based planning is really about understanding how confident we are that the client is headed in the right direction.

Diversification Explained

Diversification Explained

Diversification is a widely used term within the industry. You hear it everywhere but what does it really mean?

The dictionary, as it relates to investing, says: "the act or practice of investing in a variety of securities so that a failure or economic slump affecting one of them will not be disastrous". I would agree with the premise of that and I think we can all appreciate it. It is rarely, if ever, a good idea to have "all of your eggs in one basket". Diversification does not guarantee profit or protect against loss in declining markets.

But how do you actually do it? Is there a process? I believe there is.

Once your overall plan is completed, you need to determine how you will be diversified between stocks (equities), bonds (fixed income), cash and alternatives. As an aside, alternatives are anything that does not fall into the other (3) categories. Once you determine what percentage of your portfolio will go into each category then you must decide how to diversify within each grouping.

Cash is pretty simple. You need something with daily liquidity so a money market or savings account would qualify.

Within fixed income, I believe it is best to use a laddered portfolio. Basically, you diversify your investments by maturity date. This helps the portfolio spread out interest rate risk. For example, let's say you were allocating $100,000 to fixed income and you are going to place it within the ladder. You've decided that you want to use a 5-year time frame. You would place $20,000 in a bond due in one year, $20,000 in a bond due in two years, etc. You would have an equal amount coming due each year for the 5 years. That way, if interest rates rise in a year, then you can reinvest the proceeds of the one year bond at the new higher rates. However, if rates dropped, then you would be happy that you locked in better rates on bonds due in the future.

On the equity (stock) side of the portfolio, I believe there are five core areas for which you may want to diversify: Large Cap Growth, Large Cap Value, Small Cap Growth, Small Cap Value and International. There are two basic kinds of investors: a Growth investor and a Value investor. A growth investor buys a stock at say $10 because he thinks it will grow to $25. Maybe he is purchasing a biotech stock and they have a new drug coming out. Once the drug comes out then the revenues will rise and cause the stock price to go up. This investor is looking at the future value.

A value investor is looking for things that are "cheap" or "on sale". She might buy a stock at $10 because she thinks it is worth $20 today. A value investor looks at the current price rather than the future price.

Within growth and value, you also have different sizes of companies- small, medium and large. They tend to act differently in different environments. The prices of small/medium company stocks are generally more volatile than large company stocks. They often involve higher risks because smaller companies may lack the management expertise, financial resources, product diversification and competitive strengths to endure adverse economic conditions.

The last equity investment piece is international. All that means is that a company is not headquartered in the U.S. It does not mean they don't do business here. A very high percentage of the publicly traded companies in the world are not based in the U.S., so if you fail to include that in your portfolio, you are missing out on a lot of the opportunities. Investing in foreign markets presents certain risks not associated with domestic investments, such as currency fluctuation, political and economic instability, and different accounting standards. This may result in greater share price volatility.

I am a big believer in trying to limit as many variables as possible. Therefore, one of my core philosophies is that I am not going to "guess" as to which of the five core areas is going to do better than the rest and, in my opinion, I feel it is important to place the same amount into each area. After a year, you may want to rebalance. Of course, this applies on a client by client basis and may be different for different clients.

For example, let's say Large Cap Growth has done very well and is now 25% of the portfolio while small cap value lagged and is now 15% of the portfolio. Take 5% from Large Cap Growth and add it to small cap value. It forces you to take profits after something has done better and to add to areas when they are less expensive after they have lagged.

Remember, behavior is a key variable. We can control how much you have in each area and we can control when you rebalance. This can be done regardless of what the market does or does not do.

After you write a well thought out plan that focuses on your family goals and objectives then it becomes easier to determine the appropriate asset allocation. Once the asset allocation is in place then you could use the basic tenets discussed above to diversify. If you follow these simple steps, you will increase your chances of meeting your financial goals.

The market has no concern for how much you paid for an investment. The market is going to do what it is going to do. It is unknown. Spend time on the things that matter to you and that you can control. So often, I hear people say, "I can't sell it until it goes up higher to where I bought it." Why does your purchase price matter? It doesn't. If your portfolio is no longer allocated based on your goals, make the change. It may be for the better.

There are very few scenarios where one investment does well by itself and the rest of the market does terribly. However, there are many examples where one investment does poorly and the rest of the market does well.

I Talked to My Clients about...

I Talked to My Clients about...

I have reviewed portfolios with my clients and discussed my planning process. I also talked to one of my top clients about capital gains.

I talked with one of my long time clients and we had made some major changes to his dad's trust, which caused some capital gains. This was a multi- million dollar trust. The tax on the capital gains was not unreasonable but his CPA brought it to his attention. Total tax, in this case, was not that high in the big scheme of things. I reiterated why we made the changes- that the portfolio in its current state did not fit with his plan. Going forward there will be some adjustments but I doubt major changes like the ones we did. If his risk (tolerance) changes then the allocation will have to change. All that said, I think the structure of the portfolio is good and will continue to be good with some minor tweaks as we move forward.

This example reminds me that it is important NOT to make portfolio decisions solely based on taxes. If you did, no changes would be made and you would end up with another problem. Best examples of this are people who may have owned a tech stock or fund in the late 90s and said they couldn't sell it because of the tax implications. That decision cost them dearly when the tech stocks all cratered and crashed. Had they just adjusted their portfolio so it was not so focused in one area and paid the tax they would probably be much better off.

In my experience, it seems the diversification discussion resonates with people when you discuss at a conceptual level but loses some momentum during implementation. It is important that an advisor does not allow clients' portfolios to get too overweight in any one investment class only because of tax concerns. Heck, I hope we pay some capital gains every year because it generally means values are moving higher for my clients.

Nick Murray, well known advisor coach, has a great quote: "I will never own enough of any one thing to make a killing in it nor will I own too much of any one thing to be killed by it."

More examples of the diversification discussion are when people work for a company that ties a lot of the compensation to the company stock. It seems to be basic human behavior for people to think that the company they work for will perform better as an investment. Companies like Enron, Worldcom, Lehman Brothers and Bear Stearns really highlight this fact.

It is like "same country bias". If you are in Germany then you think the German market is the best place to invest. If you are in the U.S. then that is the best place to be, etc. "Same company bias" works the same way.

That said, there are many examples where an individual stock struggles but the market does well. There are very few examples where one individual stock does well and the rest of the market does poorly. You should stay diversified so you can spread out your opportunities and your risks.

I had another client who came in to discuss his mother's portfolio. She has owned stock in a private company for a long time that pays her a dividend each year. The dollar amount of the dividend is significant but it is basically a 2% payout which is nothing to get terribly excited about. We know little about what the company does and how they are doing other than what they send out. It has been around a long time so it has longevity, but it still concerns me. Mainly, it concerns me because it is two-thirds of her portfolio. I mentioned that we may want to look at a CRT (charitable remainder trust) so some of it could be sold without paying taxes and we could actually increase his mother's cash flow. A CRT is used as an estate planning tool. It allows property or money to be donated into the trust.

A charitable remainder trust (CRT) lets you make a substantial charitable gift now while retaining a defined income stream from the donated assets. The CRT is primarily a charitable-giving strategy with an added benefit- it lets you sell appreciated assets in the trust without incurring immediate capital gains taxes. The strategies discussed may not be suitable for your personal situation, even if it is similar to the example presented. Wells Fargo Advisors does not provide legal or tax advice. Be sure to consult with your own tax and legal advisors before taking any action that could have tax consequences. Any estate plan should be reviewed by an attorney who specializes in estate planning and is licensed to practice law in your state.

I also spoke to another client about municipal bonds in his home state. He has a better lay of the land as to what might be good and what is not. It's always, good to remind clients that while their biases can hurt them, local knowledge can actually help. Without his understanding of the hospital backing the bond, we may not even have considered it. I regularly contact other advisors and people within the firm to take advantage of their expertise in a specific area. For example, I talked to a friend who is from New York about one of the bedroom communities outside of the city. He had the knowledge and understanding to tell me if that area was solid financially or not. In my opinion this is much better information then just rationale from a ratings service like S&P or Moody's.

I Talked to My Clients Part 2...

I Talked to My Clients Part 2…

I spoke to several clients about a lot of different things. It is important to realize that the job of a valuable financial advisor is to help clients with all things related to their financial well-being.

I did a conference call with some long time clients to discuss long term care insurance. Long Term Care insurance helps to defer some of the cost of a nursing home, assisted living or even just having someone come to the house to provide some assistance. This is an important area to at least discuss and have a plan for. Insurance is essentially nothing more than leverage.

To make sure I'm continuously adding value to their lives, I tell my clients to talk to me about anything that relates to a "dollar" sign. I may not be the expert on everything, no one is, but I have contacts in a lot of areas so I am usually able to steer my clients in the right direction. Much of the time, the most important thing is to know where to go and who to talk to for specific advice in a specific area.

In many ways, I view myself as an advocate for my clients. A lot of moving parts in everyone's lives and it is important to know where to go and how to put it all together. Money is not the only thing where I offer advice. It is just the tool used to accomplish many of the goals set forth by clients.

I met with a new couple. They were referred to me by some long-time clients which I always appreciate. I am so grateful that I have such great clients who give me the opportunity to be their advisor.

This couple has two boys and one has some special needs, so that is an important consideration. He will probably always be close to them and may need help when his parents are no longer around or if something sudden were to occur. These issues certainly weigh on parents and I want to get beyond the numbers to try and help them.

We spent some time talking about the different estate and trust issues. They do not currently have a trust, which is critical for most clients and especially for someone with a child with special needs. I referred them over to several very good trust attorneys and I am confident one can help steer them in the right direction.

Something else that strikes me is the diverse group of clients I have. They cover so many industries which is great. I have retired engineers, current and former employees in the technology sector, and a lot of fellow alumni as well as many others.

I met with an attorney that I have been in contact with for a number of years. He had been promoted and I saw a note about him so lobbed out a phone call and we email from time to time. We met for lunch and his biggest concern is saving for his kids' college education. He and his wife have three children. We talked a lot about education plans, including 529 plans and Coverdell Education Savings accounts.

Everyone has similar priorities, in many ways, but the order of which is most important is always a bit different. It is very important to walk clients through the process of identifying the issues that matter to them and then prioritizing those items.

More examples of what I do for Clients

More examples of what I do for Clients

I had a client who needed some assistance with his company retirement plan. We discussed the myriad of options and determined that an individual 401k was the best fit. The new company is just two people.

While going through the planning process, I believe it is important for clients to really think about what they want to do and not "assume" they can or cannot do it. Just let me know and we can make it part of the plan.

For example, let's say a client wanted to take a private jet trip around the world. I can put it into the plan, price it out and see if that is feasible or not. Those kinds of exercises highlight for me why I am a financial advisor. It is very enjoyable to do such specific planning for my clients. Everyone is different.

One of my long time clients retired from his job after many decades. One of the biggest decisions he had to make was to either take a lump sum rollover for his retirement or to take the pension, giving up the lump sum. This is an important exercise and my planning process is very useful in being able to compare many different options. "What If" scenarios are critical to the planning process.

One of my largest households really demonstrates how many things you can do for a client. To me, there are really four pillars of wealth management: liability management, asset management, risk management and lifestyle management. Sometimes, I think it is important for clients to be reminded that I can be the point person for all of these areas and then bring in experts where appropriate.

For one client, we helped setup a private family foundation. It offered a great investment planning tool, some tax deductions and the ability to decide how future funds will be contributed. It is also nice to have an "anchor" that brings the family together on a consistent basis. Wells Fargo Advisors is not a legal or tax advisor.

I have had several clients ask me to do the "What if scenarios" for home improvements whether it be a pool, new room addition or anything else. It is imperative to know what you might be giving up in the future to gain something now and visa versa. I feel it allows my clients to make well informed decisions.

Had a discussion with a client about their plan and the market's volatility. It is critical to focus on the big picture. There are always going to be issues to deal with in the world whether they be economic, political or otherwise. There isn't a whole lot we can do about them. The attention has to be made to how assets are allocated, how we are diversified and how confident that we are headed in the right direction. While diversification does not guarantee profit or protect against loss in a declining market, strategically diversified portfolio can help provide more consistent returns through all kinds of market environments.

Understanding psychology and human behavior are an important part of an advisor's job, in my opinion. Being very clear and upfront with clients is also important.

I Believe...

I Believe...

- I believe my family should always be at the top of the list

- I believe that behavior is the most important determinant of how you do or don't do when it comes to financial planning or anything else

- I believe in focusing on the things you can control rather than on the things for which you have no impact

- I believe that if I do what is right for my clients then I will be compensated appropriately

- I believe the process is far more important than the product

- I believe in order to succeed you must fail

- I believe that it is better to do something than worry about if it was perfect or not. Done is better than perfect.

- I believe that momentum is very powerful

- I believe that things will turn out alright if you let them
- I believe that it is much more useful to be optimistic
- I believe that it is important to give back to the community
- I believe it is important to be grateful for what you have
- I believe my daughter is going to have a very positive impact on the world around her
- I believe my wife is a great mother and wife
- I believe it is important to fight for what you believe
- I believe it is important to consider different points of view to help formulate your own
- I believe it is better to give than receive
- I believe it is my job to make sure my clients follow the plan and try to avoid the "big mistake"
- I believe that clients who truly embrace my planning process should feel very good about the outcome as things move forward
- I believe that clients who do not embrace my planning process may not really be a fit for me
- I believe that all things cycle and understanding that is truly helpful (except CAL going to the Rose Bowl, it seems)
- I believe it is important to occasionally review what you believe

Disclosures

- Investing in fixed income securities involves certain risks such as market risk if sold prior to maturity and credit risk especially if investing in high yield bonds, which have lower ratings and are subject to greater volatility. All fixed income investments may be worth less than original cost upon redemption or maturity. Bond prices fluctuate inversely to changes in interest rates. Therefore, a general rise in interest rates can result in the decline of the value of your investment.

- Investing in foreign securities presents certain risks not associated with domestic investments, such as currency fluctuation, political and economic instability, and different accounting standards. This may result in greater share price volatility.

- Dividends are not guaranteed and are subject to change or elimination.

- Trust services available through banking and trust affiliates in addition to non-affiliated companies of Wells Fargo Advisors. Wells Fargo Advisors and its affiliates do not provide legal or tax advice. Any estate plan should be reviewed by an attorney who specializes in estate planning and is licensed to practice law in your state. Insurance products are available through non-bank insurance agency affiliates of Wells Fargo & Company and underwritten by non-affiliated Insurance Companies. Not available in all states.

- • Income from municipal securities is generally free from federal taxes and state taxes for residents of the issuing state. While the interest income is tax-free, capital gains, if any, will be subject to taxes. Income for some investors may be subject to the federal Alternative Minimum Tax (AMT).

- Diversification does not ensure a profit or protect against a loss in a down market.

Wells Fargo Advisors, LLC, member SIPC, is registered.

Investment and Insurance Products:

NOT FDIC- Insured

NO Bank Guarantee

MAY Lose Value

www.ingramcontent.com/pod-product-compliance
Lightning Source LLC
Chambersburg PA
CBHW021041180526
45163CB00005B/2227